The Illuminated
LANGUAGE OF FLOWERS

Over 700 flowers and plants
listed alphabetically with
their meanings

A MARSHALL LEE BOOK

HOLT, RINEHART AND WINSTON
NEW YORK

The Illuminated
LANGUAGE
of
FLOWERS

Illustrated by
KATE
GREENAWAY

with a text by
Jean Marsh

We are most grateful to Virginia Kelly for her assistance in researching the history of the language of flowers, and to Elizabeth Woodburn, K. Gregory, and Estelle Chessid for their generous help in this work. Special thanks are due to Isabel Zucker for her valuable advice and her comments on the text.

Printed in the United States of America
10 9 8 7 6 5 4 3 2 1

Library of Congress Cataloging in Publication Data

Greenaway, Kate, 1846-1901.
    The illuminated language of flowers.

    (A Marshall Lee book)
    1. Greenaway, Kate, 1846-1901. 2. Flower
language.   3.   Flowers in art.   I.   Marsh, Jean.
II.   Title.
NC242.G7A4 1978   741.9'42   78-4697
ISBN 0-03-044196-X

Contents

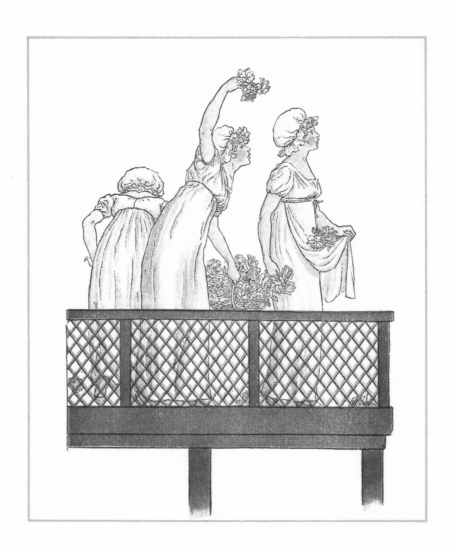

THE LANGUAGE OF FLOWERS

A Handbook for Victorian Lovers

I sent my love clematis. She, walking white
In her garden, reading Rossetti, veiled her sight
Under blue eyelids, blushingly comprehended
Her *mental beauty* was thereby commended.

My love sent me the bud of a white rose
To say *her heart knew naught of love.* Repose
Fled from my days, to tell her of my *flame*
I sent an iris. Swift her answer came;

She had gathered mouse-eared chickweed, flowers which swear
Ingenuous simplicity. Despair
Seized me, I sent gum cistus, saying: *"Tomorrow
I die."* She sent me yew, expressing *sorrow.*

True to my word, I died; and to my tomb
She mourning came. Her hat was all abloom
With rosemary, which vows *not to forget,*
And rue, to tell the world of her *regret.*

But when upon my grave, my life, my dove,
Stooped to plant myrtle, signifying *love,*
Then garden daisies in my dust were bred,
And "Sweet, *I share your sentiments,"* they said.

RANDOLPH STOW

A Manner of Speaking

JEAN MARSH

If you have ever received a single red rose from a secret admirer, you know that it was an expression of love. Imagine a thousand different messages conveyed through flowers instead of by words and you know what is meant by a language of flowers. This enchanting manner of speaking bloomed in the early nineteenth century when it became the rage to communicate specific thoughts and feelings by the exchange of carefully-composed bouquets. Hundreds of flowers and plants were given meanings that ranged from simple words like *Fidelity* (ivy) to giddy phrases such as *Your purity equals your loveliness* (orange blossom) or *First emotions of love* (purple lilac). The plant names and their meanings were compiled in dozens of "language of flowers" dictionaries that sold out one edition after another in Europe and America. And speaking of dictionaries, there is even a special word—florigraphy—that means "language of flowers." After a surprisingly difficult search for more

facts, I can now throw *some* light on this charming custom and its long and colorful history.

People have found meanings in flowers for as long as there have been flowers on the earth. I've seen a book about the discovery of Tutankhamen's tomb in which there is a strangely moving photograph of a delicate funeral bouquet that had lain in the tomb, sealed up with the dead Pharaoh, for 3500 years. The iris blossom was used as an emblem of power on the brow of the Sphinx of Giza and on the scepter of Egyptian monarchs. To ancient Romans, anemones signified love and were strewn on the altars of Venus; myths tell us that these flowers sprang up where Venus shed tears at the loss of her beloved Adonis. In the classical world, verbena was considered a symbol of peace and was present at the signing of treaties. A hint of the ancients' attitude toward the war between the sexes lies in their use of verbena at weddings! At least as early as the Middle Ages, people noticed a resemblance to the dove in the spurred, tubular petals of the columbine; as the dove stands for the Holy Spirit, so does the dove-like columbine that appears in Renaissance paintings.

For most of us, Ophelia's mournful raving in *Hamlet*—"There's rosemary, that's for remembrance"—rings a wistful note, even if we don't know that in the Middle Ages rosemary betokened remembrance because the herb was believed to improve the memory. (To me, I confess, rosemary means food, roast lamb or veal cooking slowly on a huge bed of the fresh herb.) And I wonder if Ophelia knew about the use of rue to ward off flies when she told her brother to "Wear your rue with a difference"?

The people of Shakespeare's day were at home with the plant

and flower meanings derived from ancient folklore, but the custom of a flower *language* came to Europe from the harem world of the Moslem countries. A "true story" from an American magazine of 1841 tells of a passionate romance conducted entirely in this language: A young French painter in Cairo is interrupted in his work by a child bringing a huge bouquet. On the advice of his native servant, the painter takes it to an old woman who can read its meaning for him. "This, my son," she says, "is a simple note; but from its elegance of style, it is easy to perceive that she who has written it is an author of the first merit."

The woman goes on to translate as follows: "Thou comest each day to draw the mosque and its colored stones. I behold thee, with pleasure, attentive to thy work. I envy the cupola and the minaret, because thou lookest upon them incessantly.... Not being able to speak to thee with my lips, I write with flowers. I send thee this bouquet, a messenger from my soul. May its brilliant colors, its symmetry, and its perfume, be an emblem of her who loves thee."

The correspondence continues, with larger bouquets exchanged each day, until the woman's husband—who generally neglects her for a second wife—chances to enter her boudoir. Alas, Fatma has saved her bouquets—to re-read them. While her husband runs off to an interpreter, Fatma hastily composes a floral farewell: "Dear friend! I am about to die. At midnight, when the moon is shedding her light on the city and country around, I shall be thrown into the Nile.... We shall see each other in another world where we shall continue our correspondence."

In the dénouement, there is as likely an explanation as any of how this custom travelled to Paris, which it did: the painter rescues the lady from drowning (she has been sewn into a sack with a cat and a viper) and takes her to Paris, where, the narration concludes, "She is now engaged in teaching the women of France the language of flowers."

The first real flower dictionary, *Le Langage des Fleurs,* by "Mme. Charlotte de la Tour"—actually, a woman named Louise Cortambert—was published in Paris in 1818. I don't know the source of Mme. Cortambert's ideas (unless Fatma the harem woman had already made her appearance in Paris society), but the eighteen editions of her book in French (it also appeared in pirated editions in America and Spain) attest to its popularity, as do the many other language-of-flowers books that followed it in France. Around this time, French artists were producing some of their most magnificent floral illustrations, and language-of-flowers volumes, many editions containing beautiful engravings, were another way in which publishers could meet an avid public interest in flowers and gardening.

I do know that the language-of-flowers custom was first mentioned in England by Lady Mary Wortley Montagu ("the most colourful Englishwoman of her time," according to *Encyclopedia Brittanica),* when the letters she wrote home from Constantinople were published posthumously in 1763. In 1717 she had written to a friend: "I have got for you, as you desire, a Turkish love-letter . . . the translation of it literally is as follows: The first piece you should pull out of the purse is a little pearl, which . . . must be understood in this manner:

| *Ingi* | *Sensin uzellerin gingi* |
| Pearl | Fairest of the young . . . |

Pul	*Derdime derman bul*
Jonquil	Have pity on my passion! . . .
Gul	*Ben aglarum sen gul*
A rose	May you be pleased, and your sorrows mine

. . . There is no colour, no flower, no weed, no fruit, herb, pebble, or feather that has not a verse belonging to it; and you may quarrel, reproach, or send letters of passion, friendship, or civility, or even of news, without ever inking your fingers."

It amuses me to think that Lady Mary inspired the language-of-flowers pastime—she was a figure of such a different age! "I think there are but two pleasures permitted to mortal man," she wrote at the end of her life, "love and vengeance." She envies the Turkish women their freedom: covered from head to toe by their costumes, they can meet their lovers in the streets without being recognized, even by their own husbands! A glance at the list of sentiments in this book—*Alas! for my poor heart* (deep red carnation), *Bury me among nature's beauties* (persimmon), *Fidelity in adversity* (wall-flower)—is enough to suggest the vast gulf between the Victorian sensibility and Lady Mary's far lustier preoccupations. No wall-flowers in her garden, I'd guess!

It is not surprising then, that almost immediately after the appearance of Mme. Cortambert's book in Paris, language-of-flowers dictionaries were published in English—with comparable success. The fashion for these books in England began in the days of George IV and ran through the 1840s, the early years of Queen Victoria's reign; in America, the vogue took hold a little later.

In those days, what we think of as Victorian manners and morals—upright and a little hypocritical—prevailed everywhere among people who had freshly acquired the means and the desire to lead genteel lives, but often lacked the requisite knowledge.

With the help of flower-language books, shy Victorians were able to find ways to express what they could not say in words; they sent each other bouquets in which every blossom, leaf, and stem was fraught with significance. "A party walking in a garden," the author of one of these books proclaims, "through the means of flowers presented to each other, may carry on a conversation of compliment, wit, and repartée." What a fine pastime for ladies with not quite enough to do!

In a period when gentility was valued as never before (or since), an interest in flower language lent an air of modest feminine erudition to the lady gardener, at the same time allowing her to mingle dreams of romance with more prosaic gardening concerns. Since the Victorians cultivated virtuousness rather than passion, it is not surprising that they responded to the delicate blooms of the garden.

Although the authors of language-of-flowers books sometimes alluded to the Middle Eastern origin of the custom, no one seems to have known much more of its history than what Lady Mary had reported. Henry Phillips, author of some of the best-known British volumes, provided some genuine scholarship about the meanings attributed to flowers in folklore and literature, but, more often, authors filled their books with literary and classical quotations that made references to the flowers or to the meanings the authors had chosen to assign to them.

Some authors presented their own original sentimental poetry;

some presented other people's poetry and said it was their own; many took a democratic approach that set lines from Shakespeare, Spenser, and Milton alongside the verses of poets like "Mrs. C. Smith"; and many presented no justification at all for the meanings they listed opposite the names of the flowers. Mrs. E.W. Wirt, author of *Flora's Dictionary,* one of the best-known American books of this kind, loftily declares, "It would be idle . . . to give consequence to a trifle so light and airy as this, by indicating, in every instance, the reasons which led to the selection of the emblems; these will present themselves readily to the mind of the reader." In Mrs. Wirt's book, the ivy geranium means *May I have your hand for the next quadrille?*—I wonder how many readers' minds would come up with the reasons for *that* selection?

Indeed, I wonder whether many people were brave enough to send the kinds of flower messages these books recommend. "I or me is expressed by inclining the flower to the left; thou or thee by sloping it to the right," one author advises. I immediately think: *whose* right or left? A white rose means *I am worthy of you;* a dried white rose, *Death preferable to loss of innocence.* Woe betide the suitor whose bouquet fades before his sweetheart gets a chance to read it! In Louisa May Alcott's *Jo's Boys,* a proposal of marriage is offered, and accepted, in flower language, so we know the process worked—at least in novels.

Authors and publishers did little to prevent readers' confusion: of the 150-or-so flower-language dictionaries, no two agreed completely about the meanings of the flowers, unless one happened to be plagiarized from the other. The only element linking the various dictionaries was their use of the traditional symbolic meanings of flowers that had become part of the culture and folklore of the Western

world; for example, narcissus always meant egotism. And even in a single dictionary a plant might be given three totally different, even contradictory, meanings. A bouquet recipient, left to decide which meaning was intended, probably shuddered at the thought of making the wrong choice. Considering the impracticality, if not the hazard, of relying on the contents of the dictionaries, we can assume that the real purpose of these books must have been more like the purpose of gardens themselves—to exist as things of beauty and to provide an enjoyable pastime.

I never had much time to garden until I became a "Rose"; *Upstairs, Downstairs* enabled me to be less a town mouse than a country girl. Now my garden in Oxfordshire is full of all the flowers I love best—narcissus, lily-of-the-valley, lilacs, daisies, and beds and beds of roses. The language of flowers aroused my curiosity about many flowers I had never heard of, but I must confess that my own bouquets are chosen for their beauty and scent; anyone reading between the flowers, as it were, is likely to get a garbled message, such as "I am bashful and ashamed and beauty is your only attraction" (deep red roses and Japan roses).

When I *could* turn my attention to flowers, I became a cheerfully hybridized reader of anything on the subject I could find. In that early flush of flower-book hunting I found and fell in love with a first edition of Kate Greenaway's *Language of Flowers*.

* * *

Kate Greenaway is probably the world's most-beloved children's illustrator. I adored her books and pictures as a little girl. Her first book, *Under the Windows,* was published in London in 1877, when she was thirty-three years old. It was an immediate success in Britain, and soon her popularity spread all over the world. Her work was then widely published—and frequently imitated. Her lovely drawings appeared on greeting cards and as the illustrations for about twenty books, the original editions of which are prized by collectors.

Much of Kate Greenaway's work evoked reminiscences of bygone days and a longing even for days that had never been. No children ever dressed like the immortal boys and girls who romp gently through the pages of her books—none, that is, until life imitated art and real children's clothes were made in the styles worn by her picture-book children. (Although the clothes were imaginary, the children she drew were real, and we know who some of them were. For me, there is a special nostalgia in knowing that Gertie, the pretty red-haired "Kate Greenaway girl" on page thirty-nine of this book, grew up to be Miss Greenaway's own house parlour-maid—the "Rose" in her life.)

When her lovely *Language of Flowers* was published in 1884, times had changed and the language-of-flowers fashion had passed. The book was a sentimental reminder of a custom enjoyed by its readers' grandparents. Its drawings of flowers and fruit have been called the high point of Kate Greenaway's art, and all of them are reproduced in *The Illuminated Language of Flowers.* However, the flower dictionary that she selected to accompany her illustrations had been carelessly prepared and inadequately cross-indexed. I am happy to say that in the present book the dictionary is consistent and the list-by-

18

meaning includes almost a third-again as many entries as the list Kate Greenaway used. Also, in her small volume the listings were presented in type almost too tiny to read; the flower-language captions and the verses were printed at the back of the book, not with the illustrations to which they are related.

When I first saw Kate Greenaway's drawings in *Language of Flowers* I thought they were as fresh and delicate as flowers themselves. It is a great delight to have them in this book, reproduced at last with their original color, for all to enjoy.

The Language of Flowers

LISTED ALPHABETICALLY BY PLANT NAME

A

Abatina : *Fickleness.*
Abecedary : *Volubility.*
Acacia : *Friendship.*
Acacia, Rose or White : *Elegance.*
Acacia, Yellow : *Secret love.*
Acalia : *Temperance.*
Acanthus : *The fine arts. Artifice.*
Achillea Millefolia : *War.*
Aconite (Wolfsbane) : *Misanthropy.*
Aconite-leaved Crowfoot : *Lustre.*
Adonis, Flos : *Painful recollections.*
African Marigold : *Vulgar minds.*
Agnus Castus : *Coldness. Indifference.*
Agrimony : *Thankfulness. Gratitude.*
Allspice : *Compassion.*
Almond, Common : *Stupidity. Indiscretion.*
Almond, Flowering : *Hope.*
Aloe : *Grief. Religious superstition.*
Althaea Frutex (Syrian Mallow) : *Persuasion.*
Alyssum, Sweet : *Worth beyond beauty.*
Amaranth Globe : *Immortality. Unfading love.*
Amaranth, Cockscomb : *Foppery. Affectation.*
Amaryllis : *Pride. Timidity. Splendid beauty.*
Ambrosia : *Love returned.*
American Cowslip : *Divine beauty. You are my divinity.*
American Elm : *Patriotism.*
American Linden : *Matrimony.*
American Starwort : *Welcome to a stranger. Cheerfulness in old age.*
Amethyst : *Admiration.*
Anemone (Zephyr Flower) : *Sickness. Expectation.*
Anemone, Garden : *Forsaken.*

Angelica : *Inspiration.*
Angrec : *Royalty.*
Apocynum (Dogsbane) : *Deceit.*
Apple : *Temptation.*
Apple Blossom : *Preference. Fame speaks him great and good.*
Apple, Thorn : *Deceitful charms.*
Arbor Vitae : *Unchanging friendship. Live for me.*
Arum (Wake Robin) : *Ardour.*
Ash-leaved Trumpet Flower : *Separation.*
Ash Tree : *Grandeur.*
Aspen Tree : *Lamentation.*
Asphodel : *My regrets follow you to the grave.*
Aster, China : *Variety. Afterthought.*
Auricula : *Painting.*
Auricula, Scarlet : *Avarice.*
Austurtium : *Splendour.*
Azalea : *Temperance.*

Friendship

ACACIA

Gather ye rose-buds while ye may:
Old Time is still a-flying.

Herrick

B

Bachelor's Buttons : *Celibacy.*
Balm : *Sympathy.*
Balm, Gentle : *Pleasantry.*
Balm of Gilead : *Cure. Relief.*
Balsam, Red : *Touch me not. Impatient resolves.*
Balsam, Yellow : *Impatience.*
Barberry : *Sourness of temper.*
Barberry Tree : *Sharpness.*
Basil : *Hatred.*
Bay Leaf : *I change but in death.*
Bay Tree : *Glory.*
Bay Wreath : *Reward of merit.*
Bearded Crepis : *Protection.*
Beech Tree : *Prosperity.*
Bee Orchis : *Industry.*
Bee Ophrys : *Error.*
Belladonna : *Silence.*
Bellflower, Pyramidal : *Constancy.*
Bellflower, Small White : *Gratitude.*
Belvedere : *I declare against you.*
Betony : *Surprise.*
Bilberry : *Treachery.*
Bindweed, Great : *Insinuation.*
Bindweed, Small : *Humility.*
Birch : *Meekness.*
Birdsfoot Trefoil : *Revenge.*
Bittersweet Nightshade : *Truth.*
Black Poplar : *Courage.*
Blackthorn : *Difficulty.*
Bladder Nut Tree : *Frivolity. Amusement.*

Bluebell : *Constancy.*
Bluebottle (Centaury) : *Delicacy.*
Blue-flowered Greek Valerian : *Rupture.*
Borage : *Bluntness.*
Borus Henricus : *Goodness.*
Box Tree : *Stoicism.*
Bramble : *Lowliness. Envy. Remorse.*
Branch of Currants : *You please all.*
Branch of Thorns : *Severity. Rigour.*
Bridal Rose : *Happy love.*
Broom : *Humility. Neatness.*
Buckbean : *Calm repose.*
Bud of White Rose : *Heart ignorant of love.*
Bugloss : *Falsehood.*
Bulrush : *Indiscretion. Docility.*
Bundle of Reeds (with their panicles) : *Music. Complaisance.*
Burdock : *Importunity. Touch me not.*
Buttercup (Kingcup) : *Ingratitude. Childishness. Desire for riches.*
Butterfly Orchis : *Gaiety.*
Butterfly Weed : *Let me go.*

C

Cabbage : *Profit.*
Cacalia : *Adulation.*
Cactus : *Warmth.*
Calla Aethiopica : *Magnificent beauty.*
Calycanthus : *Benevolence.*
Camellia Japonica, Red : *Unpretending excellence.*
Camellia Japonica, White : *Perfected loveliness.*
Camomile : *Energy in adversity.*
Canary Grass : *Perseverance.*
Candytuft, Everflowering : *Indifference.*
Canterbury Bell : *Acknowledgment.*

Sweet is the Rose, but growes upon a brere;
Sweet is the Juniper, but sharpe his bough;
Sweet is the Eglantine, but pricketh nere;
Sweet is the Firbloom, but his branches rough;
Sweet is the Cypress, but his rind is tough.
Sweet is the Nut, but bitter is his pill.
Sweet is the Broome-flowere, but yet sowre enough;
And sweet is Moly, but his roote is ill.
So every sweet with sowre is tempred still.
That maketh it be coveted the more:
For easie things that may be got at will,
Most sorts of men doe set but little store.
Why then should I account of little pain,
That endless pleasure shall unto me gaine?

Spenser

Amusement

BLADDER NUT TREE

Cape Jasmine : *I am too happy. Transport of joy.*
Cardamine : *Paternal error.*
Cardinal Flower : *Distinction.*
Carnation, Deep Red : *Alas! for my poor heart.*
Carnation, Striped : *Refusal.*
Carnation, Yellow : *Disdain.*
Catchfly : *Snare.*
Catchfly, Red : *Youthful love.*
Catchfly, White : *Betrayed.*
Cedar : *Strength.*
Cedar Leaf : *I live for thee.*
Cedar of Lebanon : *Incorruptible.*
Celandine, Lesser : *Joys to come.*
Centaury : *Delicacy.*
Cereus, Creeping : *Modest genius. Horror.*
Champignon (*Mushroom*) : *Suspicion.*
Chervil, Garden : *Sincerity.*
Chequered Fritillary : *Persecution.*
Cherry Tree : *Good education.*
Cherry Tree, White : *Deception.*
Chestnut Tree : *Do me justice. Luxury.*
Chickweed : *Rendezvous.*
Chicory : *Frugality.*
China Aster : *Variety.*
China Aster, Double : *I share your sentiments.*
China Aster, Single : *I will think of it.*
China or Indian Pink : *Aversion.*
China Rose : *Beauty always new.*
Chinese Chrysanthemum : *Cheerfulness under adversity.*
Christmas Rose : *Relieve my anxiety.*
Chrysanthemum, Red : *I love.*
Chrysanthemum, White : *Truth.*
Chrysanthemum, Yellow : *Slighted love.*
Cinquefoil : *Maternal affection.*
Circaea : *Spell.*
Cistus (Rock Rose) : *Popular favour.*

Cistus, Gum : *I shall die tomorrow.*
Citron : *Ill-natured beauty.*
Clematis : *Mental beauty.*
Clematis, Evergreen : *Poverty.*
Clotbur : *Rudeness. Pertinacity.*
Clover, Four-leaved : *Be mine.*
Clover, Red : *Industry.*
Clover, White : *Think of me.*
Cloves : *Dignity.*
Cobaea : *Gossip.*
Cockscomb Amaranth : *Foppery. Affectation. Singularity.*
Colchicum : *My best days are past.*
Coltsfoot : *Justice shall be done.*
Columbine : *Folly.*
Columbine, Purple : *Resolved to win.*
Columbine, Red : *Anxious and trembling.*
Convolvulus : *Bonds.*
Convolvulus, Blue (Minor) : *Repose. Night.*
Convolvulus, Major : *Extinguished hopes.*
Convolvulus, Pink : *Worth sustained by judicious and tender affection.*
Corchorus : *Impatient of absence.*
Coreopsis : *Always cheerful.*
Coreopsis Arkansa : *Love at first sight.*
Coriander : *Hidden worth.*
Corn : *Riches.*
Corn Bottle : *Delicacy.*
Corn Cockle : *Gentility.*
Corn Straw : *Agreement.*
Corn Straw, Broken : *Quarrel.*
Cornel Tree : *Duration.*
Coronella : *Success crown your wishes.*
Cowslip : *Pensiveness. Winning grace.*
Cowslip, American : *Divine beauty. You are my divinity.*

Now the bright morning-star, day's harbinger,
Comes dancing from the east, and leads with her
The flowery May, who from her green lap throws
The y llow cowslip and the pale primrose.
    Hail, bounteous May, that dost inspire
    Mirth, and youth, and warm desire;
    Woods and groves are of thy dressing,
    Hill and dale doth boast thy blessing.
Thus we salute thee with our early song,
    And welcome thee, and wish thee long.

Milton

Divine Beauty

AMERICAN COWSLIP

Cranberry : *Cure for heartache.*
Creeping Cereus : *Horror. Modest Genius.*
Cress : *Stability. Power.*
Crocus : *Abuse not.*
Crocus, Saffron : *Mirth.*
Crocus, Spring : *Youthful gladness.*
Crown Imperial : *Majesty. Power.*
Crowfoot : *Ingratitude.*
Crowfoot, Aconite-leaved : *Lustre.*
Crowsbill : *Envy.*
Cuckoo Plant : *Ardour.*
Cudweed, American : *Unceasing remembrance.*
Currant : *Thy frown will kill me.*
Cuscuta : *Meanness.*
Cyclamen : *Diffidence.*
Cypress : *Death. Mourning. Despair.*

There grew pied Wind-flowers and Violets,
Daisies, those pearl'd Arcturi of the earth,
The constellated flowers that never set;
Faint Oxlips; tender Blue-bells, at whose birth
The sod scarce heaved; and that tall flower that wets
Its mother's face with Heaven-collected tears,
When the low wind, its playmate's voice, it hears.

And in the warm hedge grew lush Eglantine,
Green Cow-bind and the moonlight-colour'd May
And cherry blossoms, and white cups, whose wine
Was the bright dew yet drained not by the day;
And Wild Roses, and Ivy serpentine
With its dark buds and leaves, wandering astray,
And flowers azure, black, and streaked with gold,
Fairer than any wakened eyes behold.

And nearer to the river's trembling edge
There grew broad flag-flowers, purple prankt with white,
And starry river buds among the sedge,
And floating Water-lilies, broad and bright,
Which lit the oak that overhung the hedge
With moonlight beams of their own watery light;
And bulrushes, and reeds of such deep green
As soothed the dazzled eye with sober sheen.

Shelley

Fade, Flow'rs! fade, Nature will have it so;
'Tis but what we must in our autumn do!
And as your leaves lie quiet on the ground,
The loss alone by those that lov'd them found;
So in the grave shall we as quiet lie,
Miss'd by some few that lov'd our company;
But some so like to thorns and nettles live,
That none for them can, when they perish, grieve.

Waller

D

Daffodil : *Regard.*
Dahlia : *Instability.*
Daisy : *Innocence.*
Daisy, Garden : *I share your sentiments.*
Daisy, Michaelmas : *Farewell. Afterthought.*
Daisy, Parti-coloured : *Beauty.*
Daisy, Wild : *I will think of it.*
Damask Rose : *Brilliant complexion. Freshness.*
Dandelion : *Rustic oracle.*
Daphne Odora : *Painting the lily.*
Darnel (Ray Grass) : *Vice.*
Dead Leaves : *Sadness.*
Dew Plant : *A serenade.*
Dittany of Crete : *Birth.*
Dittany of Crete, White : *Passion.*
Dock : *Patience.*
Dodder of Thyme : *Baseness.*
Dogsbane : *Deceit. Falsehood.*
Dogwood : *Durability.*
Dragon Plant : *Snare.*
Dragonswort : *Horror.*
Dried Flax : *Utility.*

Why do ye weep, sweet babes? Can tears
　　Speak grief in you,
　　　　Who were but born
　　　　Just as the modest morn
Teemed her refreshing dew?

Herrick

Sadness

DEAD LEAVES

F

Fennel : *Worthy of all praise. Strength.*
Fern : *Fascination.*
Ficoides (Ice Plant) : *Your looks freeze me.*
Fig : *Argument.*
Fig Marigold : *Idleness.*
Fig Tree : *Prolific.*
Filbert : *Reconciliation.*
Fir : *Time.*
Fir, Scotch : *Elevation.*
Flax : *Domestic industry. Fate. I feel your kindness.*
Flax-leaved Goldy-locks : *Tardiness.*
Fleur-de-Lis : *Flame. I burn.*
Fleur-de-Luce : *Fire.*
Flowering Fern : *Reverie.*
Flowering Reed : *Confidence in Heaven.*
Flower-of-an-Hour : *Delicate beauty.*
Fly Orchis : *Error.*

E

Ebony Tree : *Blackness.*
Eglantine (European Sweetbrier) : *Poetry. I wound to heal.*
Elder : *Zealousness.*
Elm : *Dignity.*
Enchanter's Nightshade : *Witchcraft. Sorcery.*
Endive : *Frugality.*
Eupatorium : *Delay.*
Everflowering Candytuft : *Indifference.*
Evergreen Clematis : *Poverty.*
Evergreen Thorn : *Solace in adversity.*
Everlasting : *Never-ceasing remembrance.*
Everlasting Pea : *Lasting pleasure.*

Sorcery

ENCHANTER'S NIGHTSHADE

Idleness

FIG MARIGOLD

O luve will venture in, where it daur na weel be seen,
O luve will venture in, where wisdom ance hath been.

Burns

Flytrap : *Deceit.*
Fool's Parsley : *Silliness.*
Forget Me Not : *True love. Forget me not.*
Foxglove : *Insincerity.*
Foxtail Grass : *Sporting.*
French Honeysuckle : *Rustic beauty.*
French Marigold : *Jealousy.*
French Willow : *Bravery and humanity.*
Frog Ophrys : *Disgust.*
Fuchsia, Scarlet : *Taste.*
Fuller's Teasel : *Misanthropy.*
Fumitory : *Spleen.*

G

Garden Anemone : *Forsaken.*
Garden Chervil : *Sincerity.*
Garden Daisy : *I share your sentiments.*
Garden Marigold : *Uneasiness.*
Garden Ranunculus : *You are rich in attractions.*
Garden Sage : *Esteem.*
Garland of Roses : *Reward of virtue.*
Geranium, Dark : *Melancholy.*
Geranium, Ivy : *Bridal favour.*
Geranium, Lemon : *Unexpected meeting.*
Geranium, Nutmeg : *Expected meeting.*
Geranium, Oak-leaved : *True friendship.*
Geranium, Pencilled : *Ingenuity.*
Geranium, Rose-scented : *Preference.*
Geranium, Scarlet : *Comforting. Stupidity.*
Geranium, Silver-leaved : *Recall.*
Geranium, Wild : *Steadfast piety.*
Germander Speedwell : *Facility.*
Gillyflower : *Bonds of affection.*
Glory Flower : *Glorious beauty.*
Goat's Rue : *Reason.*
Goldenrod : *Precaution.*
Gooseberry : *Anticipation.*
Gourd : *Extent. Bulkiness.*
Grape, Wild : *Charity.*
Grass : *Submission. Utility.*
Guelder Rose : *Winter. Age.*

Comfort have thou of thy merit,
Kindly unassuming spirit!
Careless of thy neighbourhood,
    Thou dost show thy pleasant face
On the moor, and in the wood,
    In the lane—there's not a place,
Howsoever mean it be,
But 'tis good enough for thee.

Wordsworth

Charity

WILD GRAPE

For the Sensitive Plant has no bright flower;
Radiance and odour are not its dower;
It loves, even like Love its deep heart is full,
It desires what it has not, the beautiful!

Shelley

H

Hand Flower Tree : *Warning.*
Harebell : *Submission. Grief.*
Hawkweed : *Quicksightedness.*
Hawthorn : *Hope.*
Hazel : *Reconciliation.*
Heath : *Solitude.*
Helenium : *Tears.*
Heliotrope : *Devotion. Faithfulness.*
Hellebore : *Scandal. Calumny.*
Helmet Flower (Monkshood) : *Chivalry. Knight-errantry.*
Hemlock : *You will be my death.*
Hemp : *Fate.*
Henbane : *Imperfection.*
Hepatica : *Confidence.*
Hibiscus : *Delicate beauty.*
Holly : *Foresight.*
Holly Herb : *Enchantment.*
Hollyhock : *Ambition. Fecundity.*
Honesty : *Honesty. Fascination.*

Honey Flower : *Love sweet and secret.*
Honeysuckle : *Generous and devoted affection.*
Honeysuckle, Coral : *The colour of my fate.*
Honeysuckle, French : *Rustic beauty.*
Hop : *Injustice.*
Hornbeam : *Ornament.*
Horse Chestnut : *Luxury.*
Hortensia : *You are cold.*
Houseleek : *Vivacity. Domestic industry.*
Houstonia : *Content.*
Hoya : *Sculpture.*
Humble Plant : *Despondency.*
Hundred-leaved Rose : *Dignity of Mind. Pride.*
Hyacinth : *Sport. Game. Play.*
Hyacinth, White : *Unobtrusive loveliness.*
Hydrangea : *A boaster. Heartlessness.*
Hyssop : *Cleanliness.*

That age is best, which is the first,
　　When youth and blood are warmer;
But being spent, the worse and worst
　　Times will succeed the former.

—Then be not coy, but use your time,
　　And while ye may, go marry;
For having lost but once your prime,
　　You may for ever tarry.

Herrick

Play

HYACINTH

I

Iceland Moss : *Health.*
Ice Plant : *Your looks freeze me.*
Imperial Montague : *Power.*
Indian Cress : *Warlike trophy.*
Indian Jasmine : *Attachment. I attach myself to you.*
Indian Pink, Double : *Always lovely.*
Indian Plum : *Privation.*
Iris : *Message.*
Iris, German : *Flame.*
Ivy : *Fidelity. Marriage.*
Ivy, Sprig of (with tendrils) : *Assiduous to please.*

O, my luve's like a red, red rose,
　That's newly sprung in June;
O, my luve's like the melodie
　That's sweetly play'd in tune.

Burns

Attachment

INDIAN JASMINE

K

Kennedia : *Mental beauty.*
Kingcup : *Desire for riches. Ingratitude. Childishness.*

J

Jacob's Ladder : *Come down.*
Japan Rose : *Beauty is your only attraction.*
Jasmine : *Amiability.*
Jasmine, Cape : *Transport of joy. I am too happy.*
Jasmine, Carolina : *Separation.*
Jasmine, Indian : *I attach myself to you. Attachment.*
Jasmine, Spanish : *Sensuality.*
Jasmine, Yellow : *Grace and elegance.*
Jonquil : *I desire a return of affection.*
Judas Tree : *Unbelief. Betrayal.*
Juniper : *Succour. Protection.*
Justicia : *The perfection of female loveliness.*

Come Down

JACOB'S LADDER

Now Nature hangs her mantle green
On every blooming tree,
And spreads her sheets o' daisies white
Out o'er the grassy lea.

Burns

Mental Beauty

KENNEDIA

L

Laburnum : *Forsaken. Pensive beauty.*
Lady's Slipper : *Capricious beauty. Win me and wear me.*
Lagerstraemia, Indian : *Eloquence.*
Lantana : *Rigour.*
Larch : *Audacity. Boldness.*
Larkspur : *Lightness. Levity.*
Larkspur, Pink : *Fickleness.*
Larkspur, Purple : *Haughtiness.*
Laurel : *Glory.*
Laurel, Common (in flower) : *Perfidy.*
Laurel, Ground : *Perseverance.*
Laurel, Mountain : *Ambition.*
Laurel-leaved Magnolia : *Dignity.*
Laurestina : *A token. I die if neglected.*
Lavender : *Distrust.*
Leaves, Dead : *Sadness.*
Lemon : *Zest.*
Lemon Blossoms : *Fidelity in love.*
Lettuce : *Coldheartedness.*
Lichen : *Dejection. Solitude.*

Lilac, Field : *Humility.*
Lilac, Purple : *First emotions of love.*
Lilac, White : *Youthful innocence.*
Lily, Day : *Coquetry.*
Lily, Imperial : *Majesty.*
Lily, White : *Purity. Sweetness. Modesty.*
Lily, Yellow : *Falsehood. Gaiety.*
Lily of the Valley : *Return of happiness.*
Lime or Linden Tree : *Conjugal love.*
Lint : *I feel my obligations.*
Liquorice, Wild : *I declare against you.*
Live Oak : *Liberty.*
Liverwort : *Confidence.*
Lobelia : *Malevolence.*
Locust Tree : *Elegance.*
Locust Tree (green) : *Affection beyond the grave.*
London Pride : *Frivolity.*
Lote Tree : *Concord.*
Lotus : *Eloquence.*
Lotus Flower : *Estranged love.*
Lotus Leaf : *Recantation.*
Love in a Mist : *Perplexity.*
Love Lies Bleeding : *Hopeless, not heartless.*
Lucern : *Life.*
Lupine : *Voraciousness. Imagination.*

Haughtiness

PURPLE LARKSPUR

The nymph must lose her female friend,
  If more admired than she—
But where will fierce contention end,
  If flowers can disagree.

Within the garden's peaceful scene
  Appear'd two lovely foes,
Aspiring to the rank of queen,
  The Lily and the Rose.

Cowper

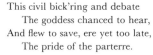

This civil bick'ring and debate
  The goddess chanced to hear,
And flew to save, ere yet too late,
  The pride of the parterre.

Yours is, she said, the nobler hue,
  And yours the statelier mien;
And, till a third surpasses you,
  Let each be deemed a queen.

Thus, soothed and reconciled, each seeks
  The fairest British fair:
The seat of empire is her cheeks,
  They reign united there.

Cowper

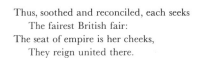
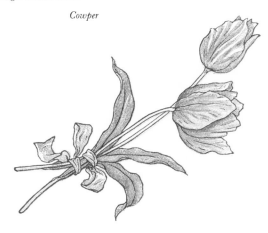

M

Madder : *Calumny.*

Magnolia : *Love of nature.*

Magnolia, Swamp : *Perseverance.*

Mallow : *Mildness.*

Mallow, Marsh : *Beneficence.*

Mallow, Syrian : *Consumed by love. Persuasion.*

Mallow, Venetian : *Delicate beauty.*

Manchineal Tree : *Falsehood.*

Mandrake : *Horror.*

Maple : *Reserve.*

Marigold : *Despair. Grief.*

Marigold, African : *Vulgar minds.*

Marigold, French : *Jealousy.*

Marigold, Prophetic : *Prediction.*

Marjoram : *Blushes.*

Marvel of Peru : *Timidity.*

Meadow Lychnis : *Wit.*

Meadow Saffron : *My happiest days are past.*

Meadowsweet : *Uselessness.*

Mercury : *Goodness.*

Mesembryanthemum : *Idleness.*

Mezereon : *Desire to please.*

Michaelmas Daisy : *Afterthought. Farewell.*

Mignionette : *Your qualities surpass your charms.*

Milfoil : *War.*

Milkvetch : *Your presence softens my pains.*

Milkwort : *Hermitage.*

Mimosa : *Sensitiveness.*

Mint : *Virtue.*

Mistletoe : *I surmount difficulties.*

Mock Orange : *Counterfeit.*

Monkshood (Helmet Flower) : *Chivalry. Knight-errantry.*

Moonwort : *Forgetfulness.*

Morning Glory : *Affectation.*

Moschatel : *Weakness.*

Moss : *Maternal love.*

Mosses : *Ennui.*

Mossy Saxifrage : *Affection.*

Motherwort : *Concealed love.*

Mountain Ash : *Prudence.*

Mourning Bride : *Unfortunate attachment. I have lost all.*

Mouse-eared Chickweed : *Ingenuous simplicity.*

Mouse-eared Scorpion Grass : *Forget me not.*

Moving Plant : *Agitation.*

Mudwort : *Tranquillity.*

Mugwort : *Happiness.*

Mulberry Tree, Black : *I shall not survive you.*

Mulberry Tree, White : *Wisdom.*

Mushroom : *Suspicion.*

Musk Plant : *Weakness.*

Mustard Seed : *Indifference.*

Myrobalan : *Privation.*

Myrrh : *Gladness.*

Myrtle : *Love.*

Maternal Love

MOSS

Alas! ye have not known that shower
　　That mars a flower:
　　　　Nor felt the unkind
　　　　Breath of a blasting wind;
　　Nor are ye worn with years;
　　Or warped as we,
　　Who think it strange to see
Such pretty flowers, like to orphans young,
Speaking by tears before ye have a tongue.

Speak, whimpering younglings, and make known
　　The reason why
　　　　Ye droop and weep.
　　　　Is it for want of sleep,
　　Or childish lullaby?
Or that ye have not seen as yet
　　The violet?
　　　　Or brought a kiss
　　　　From that sweetheart to this?
　　No, no; this sorrow shown
　　By your tears shed,
　　Would have this lecture read:
That things of greatest, so of meanest worth,
Conceived with grief are, and with tears brought forth.

Herrick

N

Narcissus : *Egotism.*
Nasturtium : *Patriotism.*
Nettle, Burning : *Slander.*
Nettle Tree : *Concert.*
Night-blooming Cereus : *Transient beauty.*
Night Convolvulus : *Night.*
Nightshade : *Truth.*

O

Oak Leaves : *Bravery.*
Oak Tree : *Hospitality.*
Oak, White : *Independence.*
Oats : *The witching soul of music.*
Oleander : *Beware.*
Olive : *Peace.*
Orange Blossom : *Your purity equals your loveliness.*
Orange Flower : *Chastity. Bridal festivities.*
Orange Tree : *Generosity.*
Orchis : *A belle.*
Osier : *Frankness.*
Osmunda : *Dreams.*
Ox Eye : *Patience.*

Concert

NETTLE TREE

Dreams

OSMUNDA

There is a garden in her face,
    Where roses and white lilies grow;
A heavenly paradise is that place,
    Wherein all pleasant fruits do grow;
There cherries grow that none may buy
Till cherry ripe themselves do cry.

Campion

P

Palm : *Victory.*
Pansy : *Thoughts.*
Parsley : *Festivity.*
Pasque Flower : *You have no claims.*
Passion Flower : *Religious superstition.*
Pea, Everlasting : *An appointed meeting. Lasting pleasure.*
Pea, Sweet : *Departure. Delicate pleasures.*
Peach : *Your qualities, like your charms, are unequalled.*
Peach Blossom : *I am your captive.*
Pear : *Affection.*
Pear Tree : *Comfort.*
Pennyroyal : *Flee away.*
Peony : *Shame. Bashfulness.*
Peppermint : *Warmth of feeling.*
Periwinkle, Blue : *Early friendship.*
Periwinkle, White : *Pleasures of memory.*
Persicaria : *Restoration.*

Persimmon : *Bury me amid nature's beauties.*
Peruvian Heliotrope : *Devotion.*
Pheasant's Eye : *Remembrance.*
Phlox : *Unanimity.*
Pigeon Berry : *Indifference.*
Pimpernel : *Change. Assignation.*
Pine : *Pity.*
Pine-apple : *You are perfect.*
Pine, Pitch : *Philosophy.*
Pine, Spruce : *Hope in adversity.*
Pink : *Boldness.*
Pink, Carnation : *Woman's love.*
Pink, Double Indian : *Always lovely.*
Pink, Double Red : *Pure and ardent love.*
Pink, Mountain : *Aspiring.*
Pink, Single Indian : *Aversion.*
Pink, Single Red : *Pure love.*
Pink, Variegated : *Refusal.*
Pink, White : *Ingeniousness. Talent.*
Plane Tree : *Genius.*
Plum, Indian : *Privation.*
Plum Tree : *Fidelity.*
Plum Tree, Wild : *Independence.*
Polyanthus : *Pride of riches.*
Polyanthus, Crimson : *The heart's mystery.*
Polyanthus, Lilac : *Confidence.*
Pomegranate : *Foolishness.*
Pomegranate Flower : *Mature elegance.*
Poplar, Black : *Courage.*
Poplar, White : *Time.*
Poppy, Red : *Consolation.*
Poppy, Scarlet : *Fantastic extravagance.*
Poppy, White : *Sleep. My bane. My antidote.*
Potato : *Benevolence.*

Early Friendship

BLUE PERIWINKLE

Now in her green mantle blithe Nature arrays,
And listens the lambkins that bleat o'er the braes,
While birds warble welcome in ilka green shaw;
But to me it's delightless—my Nannie's awa.

The snaw-drap and primrose our woodlands adorn,
And violets bathe in the weet o' the morn;
They pain my sad bosom, sae sweetly they blaw,
They mind me o' Nannie—and Nannie's awa.

Thou lav'rock that springs frae the dews of the lawn,
The shepherd to warn o' the grey-breaking dawn,
And thou mellow mavis that hails the night-fa',
Give over for pity—my Nannie's awa.

Come, autumn, sae pensive, in yellow and grey,
And sooth me wi' tidings o' Nature's decay;
The dark, dreary winter, and wild-driving snaw,
Alane can delight me—now Nannie's awa.

Burns

Prickly Pear : *Satire.*
Pride of China : *Dissension.*
Primrose : *Early youth.*
Primrose, Evening : *Inconstancy.*
Primrose, Red : *Unpatronized merit.*
Privet : *Prohibition.*
Purple Clover : *Provident.*
Pyrus Japonica : *Fairies' fire.*

Q

Quaking Grass : *Agitation.*
Quamoclit : *Busybody.*
Queen's Rocket : *You are the queen of coquettes. Fashion.*
Quince : *Temptation.*

Go, lovely Rose!
Tell her that wastes her time on me,
That now she knows,
When I resemble her to thee,
How sweet and fair she seems to be.

Waller

Fashion

QUEEN'S ROCKET

R

Ragged Robin : *Wit.*
Ranunculus : *You are radiant with charms.*
Ranunculus, Garden : *You are rich in attractions.*
Ranunculus, Wild : *Ingratitude.*
Raspberry : *Remorse.*
Ray Grass : *Vice.*
Red Catchfly : *Youthful love.*
Reed, Split : *Indiscretion.*
Reeds (with their panicles), Bundle of : *Complaisance. Music.*
Rhododendron, Rosebay : *Danger. Beware.*
Rhubarb : *Advice.*
Rocket : *Rivalry.*
Rose : *Love.*
Rose, Austrian : *Thou art all that is lovely.*
Rose, Bridal : *Happy love.*
Rose, Burgundy : *Unconscious beauty.*
Rose, Cabbage : *Ambassador of love.*
Rose, Campion : *Only deserve my love.*
Rose, Carolina : *Love is dangerous.*
Rose, China : *Beauty always new.*
Rose, Christmas : *Tranquillize my anxiety.*
Rose, Daily : *Thy smile I aspire to.*
Rose, Damask : *Brilliant complexion. Freshness.*
Rose, Deep Red : *Bashful shame.*
Rose, Full-blown (placed over two buds) : *Secrecy.*
Rose, Dog : *Pleasure and pain.*
Rose, Guelder : *Winter. Age.*
Rose, Hundred-leaved : *Pride. Dignity of mind.*
Rose, Japan : *Beauty is your only attraction.*
Rose, Maiden Blush : *If you love me, you will find it out.*
Rose, Multiflora : *Grace.*
Rose, Mundi : *Variety.*
Rose, Musk : *Capricious beauty.*

Rose, Musk (cluster) : *Charming.*
Rose, Rock : *Popular favour.*
Rose, Single : *Simplicity.*
Rose, Thornless : *Early attachment.*
Rose, Unique : *Call me not beautiful.*
Rose, White : *I am worthy of you.*
Rose, White and Red (together) : *Unity.*
Rose, White (withered) : *Transient impressions.*
Rose, Yellow : *Decrease of love. Jealousy.*
Rose, York and Lancaster : *War.*
Rosebud, Moss : *Confession of love.*
Rosebud, Red : *Pure and lovely.*
Rosebud, White : *Girlhood.*
Rosebay Rhododendron : *Beware. Danger.*
Rosemary : *Remembrance.*
Roses, Crown of : *Reward of virtue.*
Rudbeckia : *Justice.*
Rue : *Disdain.*
Rush : *Docility.*
Rye Grass : *Changeable disposition.*

Love

ROSE

Read in these Roses the sad story
Of my hard fate, and your own glory;
In the white you may discover
The paleness of a fainting lover;
In the red the flames still feeding
On my heart with fresh wounds bleeding.
The white will tell you how I languish,
And the red express my anguish,
The white my innocence displaying,
The red my martyrdom betraying;
The frowns that on your brow resided,
Have those roses thus divided.
Oh! let your smiles but clear the weather,
And then they both shall grow together.

Carew

S

Saffron : *Beware of excess.*
Saffron, Crocus : *Mirth.*
Saffron, Meadow : *My happiest days are past.*
Sage : *Domestic virtue.*
Sage, Garden : *Esteem.*
Sainfoin : *Agitation.*
Saint John's Wort : *Animosity. Superstition.*
Sardony : *Irony.*
Saxifrage, Mossy : *Affection.*
Scabious : *Unfortunate love.*
Scabious, Sweet : *Widowhood.*
Scarlet Lychnis : *Sunbeaming eyes.*
Schinus : *Religious enthusiasm.*
Scotch Fir : *Elevation.*
Sensitive Plant : *Sensibility. Delicate feelings.*
Senvy : *Indifference.*
Shamrock : *Light heartedness.*
Snakesfoot : *Horror.*
Snapdragon : *Presumption.*
Snowball : *Bound.*
Snowdrop : *Hope.*
Sorrel : *Affection.*
Sorrel, Wild : *Wit ill-timed.*
Sorrel, Wood : *Joy. Maternal tenderness.*
Southernwood : *Jest. Bantering.*
Spanish Jasmine : *Sensuality.*
Spearmint : *Warmth of sentiment.*
Speedwell : *Female fidelity.*
Speedwell, Germander : *Facility.*
Speedwell, Spiked : *Semblance.*

Spider Ophrys : *Adroitness.*
Spiderwort : *Esteem not love.*
Spiked Willow Herb : *Pretension.*
Spindle Tree : *Your charms are engraved on my heart.*
Star of Bethlehem : *Purity.*
Starwort : *Afterthought.*
Starwort, American : *Cheerfulness in old age. Welcome to a stranger.*
Stock : *Lasting beauty.*
Stock, Ten-week : *Promptness.*
Stonecrop : *Tranquillity.*
Straw, Broken : *Rupture of a contract.*
Straw, Whole : *Union.*
Strawberry Tree : *Esteem and love.*
Sumach, Venice : *Splendour. Intellectual excellence.*
Sunflower, Dwarf : *Adoration.*
Sunflower, Tall : *Haughtiness.*
Swallow-wort : *Cure for heartache.*
Sweet Basil : *Good wishes.*
Sweet Pea : *Delicate pleasures. Departure.*
Sweet Sultan : *Felicity.*
Sweet William : *Gallantry.*
Sweetbrier, American : *Simplicity.*
Sweetbrier, European : *I wound to heal. Poetry.*
Sweetbrier, Yellow : *Decrease of love.*
Sycamore : *Curiosity.*
Syringa : *Memory.*
Syringa, Carolina : *Disappointment.*

Jest

SOUTHERNWOOD

Ere a leaf is on the bush,
In the time before the thrush
Has a thought about her nest,
    Thou wilt come with half a call,
Spreading out thy glossy breast
    Like a careless prodigal;
Telling tales about the sun,
When we've little warmth, or none.

Ill befall the yellow flowers,
Children of the flaring hours!
Buttercups that will be seen,
    Whether we will see or no;
Others, too, of lofty mien,
    They have done as worldlings do,
Taken praise that should be thine,
Little, humble Celandine!

Prophet of delight and mirth,
Ill-requited upon earth;
Herald of a mighty band,
    Of a joyous train ensuing,
Serving at my heart's command,
    Tasks that are no tasks renewing;
I will sing, as doth behove,
Hymns in praise of what I love!

Wordsworth

T

Tamarisk : *Crime.*

Tansy, Wild : *I declare war against you.*

Teasel, Fuller's : *Misanthropy.*

Tendrils of Climbing Plants : *Ties.*

Thistle, Common : *Austerity.*

Thistle, Scotch : *Retaliation.*

Thorn Apple : *Deceitful charms.*

Thorn, Evergreen : *Solace in adversity.*

Thorns, Branch of : *Severity.*

Thrift : *Sympathy.*

Throatwort : *Neglected beauty.*

Thyme : *Activity.*

Tiger Flower : *For once may pride befriend me.*

Traveller's Joy : *Safety.*

Tree of Life : *Old age.*

Trefoil, Birdsfoot : *Revenge.*

Tremella Nestoc : *Resistance.*

Trillium Pictum : *Modest beauty.*

Truffle : *Surprise.*

Trumpet Flower : *Fame.*

Tuberose : *Dangerous pleasures.*

Tulip : *Fame.*

Tulip, Red : *Declaration of love.*

Tulip, Variegated : *Beautiful eyes.*

Tulip, Yellow : *Hopeless love.*

Turnip : *Charity.*

Tussilage, Sweet-scented : *Justice shall be done to you.*

Sympathy

THRIFT

Ask me why I send you here,
This firstling of the infant year;
Ask me why I send to you
This Primrose all bepearled with dew;
I straight will whisper in your ears,
The sweets of love are washed with tears.

Carew

V

Valerian : *An accommodating disposition.*
Valerian, Blue-flowered Greek : *Rupture.*
Venice Sumach : *Intellectual excellence. Splendour.*
Venus' Car : *Fly with me.*
Venus' Looking-glass : *Flattery.*
Venus' Trap : *Deceit.*
Vernal Grass : *Poor, but happy.*
Veronica : *Fidelity.*
Vervain : *Enchantment.*
Vine : *Intoxication.*
Violet, Blue : *Faithfulness.*
Violet, Dame : *Watchfulness.*
Violet, Sweet : *Modesty.*
Violet, Yellow : *Rural happiness.*
Virginian Spiderwort : *Momentary happiness.*
Virgin's Bower : *Filial love.*
Volkamenia : *May you be happy.*

W

Wake Robin : *Ardour.*
Walnut : *Intellect. Stratagem.*
Wall-flower : *Fidelity in adversity.*
Water Lily : *Purity of heart.*
Water Melon : *Bulkiness.*
Wax Plant : *Susceptibility.*
Wheat Stalk : *Riches.*
Whin : *Anger.*
White Lily : *Purity. Modesty.*
White Mullein : *Good nature.*
White Oak : *Independence.*
White Pink : *Talent.*
White Poplar : *Time.*
White Rose (dried) : *Death preferable to loss of innocence.*
Whortleberry : *Treason.*
Willow, Creeping : *Love forsaken.*
Willow, French : *Bravery and humanity.*
Willow Herb, Spiked : *Pretension.*
Willow, Water : *Freedom.*
Willow, Weeping : *Mourning.*
Winter Cherry : *Deception.*
Witch Hazel : *A spell.*
Wolfsbane : *Misanthropy.*
Woodbine : *Fraternal love.*
Wood Sorrel : *Joy. Maternal tenderness.*
Wormwood : *Absence.*

Fidelity

VERONICA

As fair art thou, my bonnie lass,
    So deep in luve am I;
And I will luve thee still, my dear,
    Till a' the seas gang dry.

Burns

Joy

WOOD SORREL

Radiant sister of the day
Awake! arise! and come away!
To the wild woods and the plains,
To the pools where winter rains
Image all their roof of leaves,
Where the pine its garland weaves
Of sapless green, and ivy dun,
Round stems that never kiss the sun.

Shelley

Xanthium : *Rudeness. Pertinacity.*
Xeranthemum : *Cheerfulness under adversity.*

Cauld blew the bitter-biting north
Upon thy early, humble birth;
Yet cheerfully thou glinted forth
    Amid the storm,
Scarce rear'd above the parent earth
    Thy tender form.

Burns

*Cheerfulness
under Adversity*

XERANTHEMUM

Y

Yew : *Sorrow.*

Z

Zephyr Flower : *Expectation.*
Zinnia : *Thoughts of absent friends.*

Sorrow

YEW

Expectation

ZEPHYR FLOWER

Fair pledges of a fruitful tree.

Herrick

The Language of Flowers

LISTED ALPHABETICALLY BY MEANING

a

Absence : *Wormwood.*

Abuse not : *Crocus*

Accommodating disposition : *Valerian*

Acknowledgment : *Canterbury Bell.*

Activity : *Thyme.*

Admiration : *Amethyst.*

Adoration : *Dwarf Sunflower.*

Adroitness : *Spider Ophrys.*

Adulation : *Cacalia.*

Advice : *Rhubarb.*

Affectation : *Cockscomb Amaranth. Morning Glory.*

Affection : *Mossy Saxifrage. Pear. Sorrel.*

Affection beyond the grave : *Locust Tree (green).*

Affection, maternal : *Cinquefoil.*

Afterthought : *China Aster. Michaelmas Daisy. Starwort.*

Age : *Guelder Rose.*

Agitation : *Moving Plant (Quaking Grass). Sainfoin.*

Agreement : *Corn Straw.*

Alas! for my poor heart : *Deep Red Carnation.*

Always cheerful : *Coreopsis.*

Always lovely : *Double Indian Pink.*

Ambassador of love : *Cabbage Rose.*

Ambition : *Hollyhock. Mountain Laurel.*

Amiability : *Jasmine.*

Amusement : *Bladder Nut Tree.*

Anger : *Whin.*

Animosity : *Saint John's Wort.*

Anticipation : *Gooseberry.*
Anxious and trembling : *Red Columbine.*
Appointed meeting : *Everlasting Pea.*
Ardour : *Arum (Wake Robin). Cuckoo Plant.*
Argument : *Fig.*
Arts or artifice : *Acanthus.*
Aspiring : *Mountain Pink.*
Assiduous to please : *Sprig of Ivy (with tendrils).*
Assignation : *Pimpernel.*
Attachment : *Indian Jasmine.*
Audacity : *Larch.*
Austerity : *Common Thistle.*
Avarice : *Scarlet Auricula.*
Aversion : *China or Indian Pink.*

b

Bantering : *Southernwood.*
Baseness : *Dodder of Thyme.*
Bashfulness : *Peony.*
Bashful shame : *Deep Red Rose.*
Beautiful eyes : *Variegated Tulip.*
Beauty : *Parti-coloured Daisy.*
Beauty always new : *China Rose.*
Beauty, capricious : *Lady's Slipper. Musk Rose.*
Beauty, delicate : *Flower-of-an-Hour. Hibiscus. Venetian Mallow.*

Beauty, divine : *American Cowslip.*
Beauty, glorious : *Glory Flower.*
Beauty, lasting : *Stock.*
Beauty, magnificent : *Calla Aethiopica.*
Beauty, mental : *Clematis. Kennedia.*
Beauty, modest : *Trillium Pictum.*
Beauty, neglected : *Throatwort.*
Beauty, pensive : *Laburnum.*
Beauty, rustic : *French Honeysuckle.*
Beauty, unconscious : *Burgundy Rose.*
Beauty is your only attraction : *Japan Rose.*
Belle : *Orchis.*
Be mine : *Four-leaved Clover.*
Beneficence : *Marsh Mallow.*
Benevolence : *Calycanthus. Potato.*
Betrayal : *Judas Tree.*
Betrayed : *White Catchfly.*
Beware : *Oleander. Rosebay Rhododendron.*
Beware of excess : *Saffron.*
Birth : *Dittany of Crete.*
Blackness : *Ebony Tree.*
Bluntness : *Borage.*
Blushes : *Marjoram.*
Boaster : *Hydrangea.*
Boldness : *Larch. Pink.*
Bonds : *Convolvulus.*
Bonds of affection : *Gillyflower.*
Bound : *Snowball.*

Bravery : *Oak Leaves.*
Bravery and humanity : *French Willow.*
Bridal favour : *Ivy Geranium.*
Bridal festivities : *Orange Flower.*
Brilliant complexion : *Damask Rose.*
Bulkiness : *Water Melon. Gourd.*
Bury me amid nature's beauties : *Persimmon.*
Busybody : *Quamoclit.*

C

Call me not beautiful : *Unique Rose.*
Calm repose : *Buckbean.*
Calumny : *Hellebore. Madder.*
Capricious beauty : *Lady's Slipper. Musk Rose.*
Celibacy : *Bachelor's Buttons.*
Change : *Pimpernel.*
Changeable disposition : *Rye Grass.*
Charity : *Turnip. Wild Grape.*
Charming : *Cluster of Musk Roses.*
Charms, deceitful : *Thorn Apple.*
Chastity : *Orange Flower.*
Cheerfulness in old age : *American Starwort.*
Cheerfulness under adversity : *Chinese Chrysanthemum. Xeranthemum.*
Childishness : *Buttercup (Kingcup).*
Chivalry : *Monkshood (Helmet Flower).*
Cleanliness : *Hyssop.*

Coldheartedness : *Lettuce.*
Coldness : *Agnus Castus.*
Colour of my fate : *Coral Honeysuckle.*
Come down : *Jacob's Ladder.*
Comfort : *Pear Tree.*
Comforting : *Scarlet Geranium.*
Compassion : *Allspice.*
Complaisance : *Bundle of Reeds (with their panicles).*
Concealed love : *Motherwort.*
Concert : *Nettle Tree.*
Concord : *Lote Tree.*
Confession of love : *Moss Rosebud.*
Confidence : *Hepatica. Lilac Polyanthus. Liverwort.*
Confidence in Heaven : *Flowering Reed.*
Conjugal love : *Lime or Linden Tree.*
Consolation : *Red Poppy.*
Constancy : *Bluebell. Pyramidal Bellflower.*
Consumed by love : *Syrian Mallow.*
Content : *Houstonia.*
Coquetry : *Day Lily.*
Counterfeit : *Mock Orange.*
Courage : *Black Poplar.*
Crime : *Tamarisk.*
Cure : *Balm of Gilead.*
Cure for heartache : *Cranberry. Swallow-wort.*
Curiosity : *Sycamore.*

d

8

Danger : *Rosebay Rhododendron.*
Dangerous pleasures : *Tuberose.*
Death : *Cypress.*
Death preferable to loss of
    innocence : *Dried White Rose.*
Deceit : *Apocynum (Dogsbane). Flytrap. Venus'*
    Trap.
Deceitful charms : *Thorn Apple.*
Deception : *White Cherry Tree. Winter*
    Cherry.
Declaration of love : *Red Tulip.*
Decrease of love : *Yellow Rose. Yellow*
    Sweetbrier.
Dejection : *Lichen.*
Delay : *Eupatorium.*
Delicacy : *Bluebottle (Centaury). Corn Bottle.*
Delicate beauty : *Flower-of-an-Hour.*
    Hibiscus. Venetian Mallow.
Delicate feelings : *Sensitive Plant.*
Delicate pleasures : *Sweet Pea.*
Departure : *Sweet Pea.*
Desire for riches : *Kingcup.*
Desire to please : *Mezereon.*
Despair : *Cypress. Marigold.*
Despondency : *Humble Plant.*
Devotion : *Heliotrope. Peruvian Heliotrope.*
Difficulty : *Blackthorn.*
Diffidence : *Cyclamen.*

Dignity : *Cloves. Elm. Laurel-leaved Magnolia.*
Dignity of mind : *Hundred-leaved Rose.*
Disappointment : *Carolina Syringa.*
Disdain : *Yellow Carnation. Rue.*
Disgust : *Frog Ophrys.*
Dissension : *Pride of China.*
Distinction : *Cardinal Flower.*
Distrust : *Lavender.*
Divine beauty : *American Cowslip.*
Docility : *Rush. Bulrush.*
Do me justice : *Chestnut Tree*
Domestic industry : *Flax. Houseleek.*
Domestic virtue : *Sage.*
Dreams : *Osmunda.*
Durability : *Dogwood.*
Duration : *Cornel Tree.*

e

Early attachment : *Thornless Rose.*
Early friendship : *Blue Periwinkle.*
Early youth : *Primrose.*
Egotism : *Narcissus*
Elegance : *Rose or White Acacia. Locust Tree.*
Elegance and grace : *Yellow Jasmine.*
Elevation : *Scotch Fir.*
Eloquence : *Indian Lagerstraemia. Lotus.*
Enchantment : *Holly Herb. Vervain.*
Energy in adversity : *Camomile.*

Ennui : *Mosses.*
Envy : *Bramble. Crowsbill.*
Error : *Bee Ophrys. Fly Orchis.*
Esteem : *Garden Sage.*
Esteem and love : *Strawberry Tree.*
Esteem not love : *Spiderwort.*
Estranged love : *Lotus Flower.*
Excellence, Unpretending : *Red Camellia Japonica.*
Expectation : *Anemone (Zephyr Flower).*
Expected meeting : *Nutmeg Geranium.*
Extent : *Gourd.*
Extinguished hopes : *Major Convolvulus.*

f

Facility : *Germander Speedwell.*
Fairies' fire : *Pyrus Japonica.*
Faithfulness : *Blue Violet. Heliotrope.*
Falsehood : *Bugloss. Dogsbane. Manchineal Tree. Yellow Lily.*
Fame : *Tulip. Trumpet Flower.*
Fame speaks him great and good : *Apple Blossom.*
Fantastic extravagance : *Scarlet Poppy.*
Farewell : *Michaelmas Daisy.*
Fascination : *Fern. Honesty.*
Fashion : *Queen's Rocket.*
Fate : *Flax. Hemp.*
Fecundity : *Hollyhock.*

Felicity : *Sweet Sultan.*
Female fidelity : *Speedwell.*
Festivity : *Parsley.*
Fickleness : *Abatina. Pink Larkspur.*
Fidelity : *Ivy. Plum Tree. Veronica.*
Fidelity in adversity : *Wall-flower.*
Fidelity in love : *Lemon Blossoms.*
Filial love : *Virgin's Bower.*
Fire : *Fleur-de-Luce.*
First emotions of love : *Purple Lilac.*
Flame : *Fleur-de-Lis. German Iris.*
Flattery : *Venus' Looking-glass.*
Flee away : *Pennyroyal.*
Fly with me : *Venus' Car.*
Folly : *Columbine.*
Foolishness : *Pomegranate.*
Foppery : *Cockscomb Amaranth.*
Foresight : *Holly.*
Forgetfulness : *Moonwort.*
Forget me not : *Forget Me Not. Mouse-eared Scorpion Grass.*
For once may pride befriend me : *Tiger Flower.*
Forsaken : *Garden Anemone. Laburnum.*
Frankness : *Osier.*
Fraternal love : *Woodbine.*
Freedom : *Water Willow.*
Freshness : *Damask Rose.*

g

Friendship : *Acacia.*
Friendship, early : *Blue Periwinkle.*
Friendship, true : *Oak-leaved Geranium.*
Friendship, unchanging : *Arbor Vitae.*
Frivolity : *Bladder Nut Tree. London Pride.*
Frugality : *Chicory. Endive.*

Gaiety : *Butterfly Orchis. Yellow Lily.*
Gallantry : *Sweet William.*
Game : *Hyacinth.*
Generosity : *Orange Tree.*
Generous and devoted affection :
    Honeysuckle.
Genius : *Plane Tree.*
Gentility : *Corn Cockle.*
Girlhood : *White Rosebud.*
Gladness : *Myrrh.*
Glorious beauty : *Glory Flower.*
Glory : *Bay Tree. Laurel.*
Good education : *Cherry Tree.*
Good nature : *White Mullein.*
Good wishes : *Sweet Basil.*
Goodness : *Borus Henricus. Mercury.*
Gossip : *Cobaea.*
Grace : *Multiflora Rose.*
Grace and elegance : *Yellow Jasmine.*
Grandeur : *Ash Tree.*

h

Gratitude : *Agrimony. Small White Bellflower.*
Grief : *Aloe. Harebell. Marigold.*

Happiness : *Mugwort*
Happy love : *Bridal Rose.*
Hatred : *Basil.*
Haughtiness : *Purple Larkspur. Tall Sunflower.*
Health : *Iceland Moss.*
Heart ignorant of love : *Bud of White Rose.*
Heartlessness : *Hydrangea.*
Hermitage : *Milkwort.*
Hidden worth : *Coriander.*
Honesty : *Honesty.*
Hope : *Flowering Almond. Hawthorn.*
    Snowdrop.
Hope in adversity : *Spruce Pine.*
Hopeless love : *Yellow Tulip.*
Hopeless, not heartless : *Love Lies Bleeding.*
Horror : *Creeping Cereus. Mandrake.*
    Dragonswort. Snakesfoot.
Hospitality : *Oak Tree.*
Humility : *Broom. Field Lilac. Small*
    Bindweed.

i

I am too happy : *Cape Jasmine.*
I am your captive : *Peach Blossom.*

I am worthy of you : *White Rose.*

I attach myself to you : *Indian Jasmine.*

I burn : *Fleur-de-Lis.*

I change but in death : *Bay Leaf.*

I declare against you : *Belvedere. Wild Liquorice.*

I declare war against you : *Wild Tansy.*

I desire a return of affection : *Jonquil.*

I die if neglected : *Laurestina.*

I feel my obligations : *Lint.*

I feel your kindness : *Flax.*

I have lost all : *Mourning Bride.*

I live for thee : *Cedar Leaf.*

I love : *Red Chrysanthemum.*

I shall die tomorrow : *Gum Cistus.*

I shall not survive you : *Black Mulberry Tree.*

I share your sentiments : *Double China Aster. Garden Daisy.*

I surmount difficulties : *Mistletoe.*

I will think of it : *Single China Aster. Wild Daisy.*

I wound to heal : *Eglantine (European Sweetbrier).*

Idleness : *Fig Marigold. Mesembryanthemum.*

If you love me, you will find it out : *Maiden Blush Rose.*

Ill-natured beauty : *Citron.*

Imagination : *Lupine.*

Immortality : *Amaranth Globe.*

Impatience : *Yellow Balsam.*

Impatient of absence : *Corchorus.*

Impatient resolves. : *Red Balsam.*

Imperfection : *Henbane.*

Importunity : *Burdock.*

Inconstancy : *Evening Primrose.*

Incorruptible : *Cedar of Lebanon.*

Independence : *Wild Plum Tree. White Oak.*

Indifference : *Agnus Castus. Everflowering Candytuft. Mustard Seed. Pigeon Berry. Senvy.*

Indiscretion : *Bulrush. Common Almond. Split Reed.*

Industry : *Bee Orchis. Red Clover.*

Industry, domestic : *Flax. Houseleek.*

Ingeniousness : *White Pink.*

Ingenuity : *Pencilled Geranium.*

Ingenuous simplicity : *Mouse-eared Chickweed.*

Ingratitude : *Buttercup (Kingcup). Crowfoot. Wild Ranunculus.*

Injustice : *Hop.*

Innocence : *Daisy.*

Insincerity : *Foxglove.*

Insinuation : *Great Bindweed.*

Inspiration : *Angelica.*

Instability : *Dahlia.*

Intellect : *Walnut.*

j

k

l

Intellectual excellence : *Venice Sumach.*
Intoxication : *Vine.*
Irony : *Sardony.*

Jealousy : *French Marigold. Yellow Rose.*
Jest : *Southernwood.*
Joy : *Wood Sorrel.*
Joys to come : *Lesser Celandine.*
Justice : *Rudbeckia.*
Justice shall be done : *Coltsfoot.*
Justice shall be done to you : *Sweet-scented Tussilage.*

Knight-errantry : *Helmet Flower (Monkshood).*

Lamentation : *Aspen Tree.*
Lasting beauty : *Stock.*
Lasting pleasure : *Everlasting Pea.*
Let me go : *Butterfly Weed.*
Levity : *Larkspur.*
Liberty : *Live Oak.*
Life : *Lucern.*
Lightheartedness : *Shamrock.*
Lightness : *Larkspur.*

m

Live for me : *Arbor Vitae.*
Love : *Myrtle. Rose.*
Love at first sight : *Coreopsis Arkansa.*
Love forsaken : *Creeping Willow.*
Love is dangerous : *Carolina Rose.*
Love of nature : *Magnolia.*
Love returned : *Ambrosia.*
Love sweet and secret : *Honey Flower.*
Lowliness : *Bramble.*
Lustre : *Aconite-leaved Crowfoot.*
Luxury : *Chestnut Tree (Horse Chestnut).*

Magnificent beauty : *Calla Aethiopica.*
Majesty : *Crown Imperial. Imperial Lily.*
Malevolence : *Lobelia.*
Marriage : *Ivy.*
Maternal affection : *Cinquefoil.*
Maternal love : *Moss.*
Maternal tenderness : *Wood Sorrel.*
Matrimony : *American Linden.*
Mature elegance : *Pomegranate Flower.*
May you be happy : *Volkamenia.*
Meanness : *Cuscuta.*
Meekness : *Birch.*
Melancholy : *Dark Geranium.*
Memory : *Syringa.*
Mental beauty : *Clematis. Kennedia.*

Message : *Iris.*
Mildness : *Mallow.*
Mirth : *Saffron Crocus.*
Misanthropy : *Aconite (Wolfsbane). Fuller's Teasel.*
Modest beauty : *Trillium Pictum.*
Modest genius : *Creeping Cereus.*
Modesty : *Sweet Violet. White Lily.*
Momentary happiness : *Virginian Spiderwort.*
Mourning : *Cypress. Weeping Willow.*
Music : *Bundle of Reeds (with their panicles).*
My antidote : *White Poppy.*
My bane : *White Poppy.*
My best days are past : *Colchicum.*
My happiest days are past : *Meadow Saffron.*
My regrets follow you to the grave : *Asphodel.*

Neatness : *Broom.*
Neglected beauty : *Throatwort.*
Never-ceasing remembrance : *Everlasting.*
Night : *Blue (Minor) Convolvulus. Night Convolvulus.*

Old age : *Tree of Life.*
Only deserve my love : *Campion Rose.*
Ornament : *Hornbeam.*

Painful recollections : *Flos Adonis.*
Painting : *Auricula.*
Painting the lily : *Daphne Odora.*
Passion : *White Dittany of Crete.*
Paternal error : *Cardamine.*
Patience : *Dock. Ox Eye.*
Patriotism : *American Elm. Nasturtium.*
Peace : *Olive.*
Pensive beauty : *Laburnum.*
Pensiveness : *Cowslip.*
Perfected loveliness : *White Camellia Japonica.*
Perfidy : *Common Laurel (in flower).*
Perplexity : *Love in a Mist.*
Persecution : *Chequered Fritillary.*
Perseverance : *Canary Grass. Ground Laurel. Swamp Magnolia.*
Persuasion : *Althea Frutex. Syrian Mallow.*
Pertinacity : *Clotbur. Xanthium.*
Philosophy : *Pitch Pine.*
Pity : *Pine*
Play : *Hyacinth.*
Pleasantry : *Gentle Balm.*
Pleasure and pain : *Dog Rose.*
Pleasure, lasting : *Everlasting Pea.*
Pleasures of memory : *White Periwinkle.*
Poetry : *Eglantine (European Sweetbrier).*
Poor, but happy : *Vernal Grass.*

p

73

n

o

Popular favour : *Cistus (Rock Rose)*.
Poverty : *Evergreen Clematis*.
Power : *Crown Imperial. Imperial Montague.*
    Cress.
Precaution : *Goldenrod.*
Prediction : *Prophetic Marigold.*
Preference : *Apple Blossom. Rose-scented*
    Geranium.
Presumption : *Snapdragon.*
Pretension : *Spiked Willow Herb.*
Pride : *Amaryllis. Hundred-leaved Rose.*
Pride of riches : *Polyanthus.*
Privation : *Indian Plum. Myrobalan.*
Profit : *Cabbage.*
Prohibition : *Privet.*
Prolific : *Fig Tree.*
Promptness : *Ten-week Stock.*
Prosperity : *Beech Tree.*
Protection : *Bearded Crepis. Juniper.*
Provident : *Purple Clover.*
Prudence : *Mountain Ash.*
Pure love : *Single Red Pink.*
Pure and ardent love : *Double Red Pink.*
Pure and lovely : *Red Rosebud.*
Purity : *Star of Bethlehem. White Lily.*
Purity of heart : *Water Lily.*

Quarrel : *Broken Corn Straw.*
Quicksightedness : *Hawkweed.*

q

Reason : *Goat's Rue.*
Recall : *Silver-leafed Geranium.*
Recantation : *Lotus Leaf.*
Reconciliation : *Filbert. Hazel.*
Refusal : *Striped Carnation. Variegated Pink.*
Regard : *Daffodil.*
Relief : *Balm of Gilead.*
Relieve my anxiety : *Christmas Rose.*
Religious enthusiasm : *Schinus.*
Religious superstition : *Aloe. Passion Flower.*
Remembrance : *Pheasant's Eye. Rosemary.*
Remorse : *Bramble. Raspberry.*
Rendezvous : *Chickweed.*
Repose : *Blue (Minor) Convolvulus.*
Reserve : *Maple.*
Resistance : *Tremella Nestoc.*
Resolved to win : *Purple Columbine.*
Restoration : *Persicaria.*
Retaliation : *Scotch Thistle.*
Return of happiness : *Lily of the Valley.*
Revenge : *Birdsfoot Trefoil.*
Reverie : *Flowering Fern.*
Reward of merit : *Bay Wreath.*
Reward of virtue : *Garland of Roses.*

r

Riches : *Corn (Wheat Stalk)*.
Rigour : *Branch of Thorns. Lantana*.
Rivalry : *Rocket*.
Royalty : *Angrec*.
Rudeness : *Clotbur. Xanthium*.
Rupture : *Blue-flowered Greek Valerian*.
Rupture of a contract : *Broken Straw*.
Rural happiness : *Yellow Violet*.
Rustic beauty : *French Honeysuckle*.
Rustic oracle : *Dandelion*.

s

Sadness : *Dead Leaves*.
Safety : *Traveller's Joy*.
Satire : *Prickly Pear*.
Scandal : *Hellebore*.
Sculpture : *Hoya*.
Secrecy : *Full-blown Rose (placed over two buds)*.
Secret love : *Yellow Acacia*.
Semblance : *Spiked Speedwell*.
Sensibility : *Sensitive Plant*.
Sensitiveness : *Mimosa*.
Sensuality : *Spanish Jasmine*.
Separation : *Ash-leaved Trumpet Flower. Carolina Jasmine*.
Serenade : *Dew Plant*.
Severity : *Branch of Thorns*.

Shame : *Peony*.
Sharpness : *Barberry Tree*.
Sickness : *Anemone (Zephyr Flower)*.
Silence : *Belladonna*.
Silliness : *Fool's Parsley*.
Simplicity : *American Sweetbrier. Single Rose*.
Sincerity : *Garden Chervil*.
Singularity : *Cockscomb Amaranth*.
Slander : *Burning Nettle*.
Sleep : *White Poppy*.
Slighted love : *Yellow Chrysanthemum*.
Snare : *Catchfly. Dragon Plant*.
Solace in adversity : *Evergreen Thorn*.
Solitude : *Heath. Lichen*.
Sorcery : *Enchanter's Nightshade*.
Sorrow : *Yew*.
Sourness of temper : *Barberry*.
Spell : *Circaea. Witch Hazel*.
Spleen : *Fumitory*.
Splendid beauty : *Amaryllis*.
Splendour : *Austurtium. Venice Sumach*.
Sport : *Hyacinth*.
Sporting : *Foxtail Grass*.
Stability : *Cress*.
Steadfast piety : *Wild Geranium*.
Stoicism : *Box Tree*.
Stratagem : *Walnut*.
Strength : *Cedar. Fennel*.

Stupidity : *Common Almond. Scarlet Geranium.*
Submission : *Grass. Harebell.*
Success crown your wishes : *Coronella.*
Succour : *Juniper.*
Sunbeaming eyes : *Scarlet Lychnis.*
Superstition : *Saint John's Wort.*
Surprise : *Betony. Truffle.*
Susceptibility : *Wax Plant.*
Suspicion : *Champignon (Mushroom).*
Sweetness : *White Lily.*
Sympathy : *Balm. Thrift.*

t

Talent : *White Pink.*
Tardiness : *Flax-leaved Goldy-locks.*
Taste : *Scarlet Fuchsia.*
Tears : *Helenium.*
Temperance : *Acalia. Azalea.*
Temptation : *Apple. Quince.*
Thankfulness : *Agrimony.*
The colour of my fate : *Coral Honeysuckle.*
The heart's mystery : *Crimson Polyanthus.*
The perfection of female
    loveliness : *Justicia.*
The witching soul of music : *Oats.*
Think of me : *White clover.*
Thou art all that is lovely : *Austrian Rose.*
Thoughts : *Pansy.*

Thoughts of absent friends : *Zinnia.*
Thy frown will kill me : *Currant.*
Thy smile I aspire to : *Daily Rose.*
Ties : *Tendrils of Climbing Plants.*
Time : *Fir. White Poplar.*
Timidity : *Amaryllis. Marvel of Peru.*
Token : *Laurestina.*
Touch me not : *Burdock. Red Balsam.*
Tranquillity : *Mudwort. Stonecrop.*
Tranquillize my anxiety : *Christmas Rose.*
Transient beauty : *Night-blooming Cereus.*
Transient impressions : *Withered White Rose.*
Transport of joy : *Cape Jasmine.*
Treachery : *Bilberry.*
Treason : *Whortleberry.*
True friendship : *Oak-leaved Geranium.*
True love : *Forget Me Not.*
Truth : *Bittersweet Nightshade. Nightshade.*
    White Chrysanthemum.

u

Unanimity : *Phlox.*
Unbelief : *Judas Tree.*
Unceasing remembrance : *American*
    Cudweed.
Unchanging friendship : *Arbor Vitae.*
Unconscious beauty : *Burgundy Rose.*
Uneasiness : *Garden Marigold.*

Unexpected meeting : *Lemon Geranium.*
Unfading love : *Amaranth Globe.*
Unfortunate attachment : *Mourning Bride.*
Unfortunate love : *Scabious.*
Union : *Whole Straw.*
Unity : *White and Red Rose together.*
Unobtrusive loveliness : *White Hyacinth.*
Unpatronized merit : *Red Primrose.*
Unpretending excellence : *Red Camellia Japonica.*
Uselessness : *Meadowsweet.*
Utility : *Dried Flax. Grass.*

V

Variety : *China Aster. Mundi Rose.*
Vice : *Darnel (Ray Grass).*
Victory : *Palm.*
Virtue : *Mint.*
Virtue, domestic : *Sage.*
Vivacity : *Houseleek.*
Volubility : *Abecedary.*
Voraciousness : *Lupine.*
Vulgar minds : *African Marigold.*

W

War : *Achillea Millefolia. Milfoil. York and Lancaster Rose.*
Warlike trophy : *Indian Cress.*

Warmth : *Cactus.*
Warmth of feeling : *Peppermint.*
Warmth of sentiment : *Spearmint.*
Warning : *Hand Flower Tree.*
Watchfulness : *Dame Violet.*
Weakness : *Moschatel. Musk Plant.*
Welcome to a stranger : *American Starwort.*
Widowhood : *Sweet Scabious.*
Win me and wear me : *Lady's Slipper.*
Winning grace : *Cowslip.*
Winter : *Guelder Rose.*
Wisdom : *White Mulberry Tree.*
Wit : *Meadow Lychnis. Ragged Robin.*
Wit ill-timed : *Wild Sorrel.*
Witchcraft : *Enchanter's Nightshade.*
Woman's love : *Carnation Pink.*
Worth beyond beauty : *Sweet Alyssum.*
Worth sustained by judicious and tender affection : *Pink Convolvulus.*
Worthy of all praise : *Fennel.*

Y

You are cold : *Hortensia.*
You are my divinity : *American Cowslip.*
You are perfect : *Pine-apple.*
You are radiant with charms : *Ranunculus.*
You are rich in attractions : *Garden Ranunculus.*

You are the queen of coquettes : *Queen's Rocket.*
You have no claims : *Pasque Flower.*
You please all : *Branch of Currants.*
You will be my death : *Hemlock.*
Your charms are engraven on my heart : *Spindle Tree.*
Your looks freeze me : *Ice Plant.*
Your presence softens my pains : *Milkvetch.*
Your purity equals your loveliness : *Orange Blossom.*

Your qualities, like your charms, are unequalled : *Peach.*
Your qualities surpass your charms : *Mignionette.*
Youthful gladness : *Spring Crocus.*
Youthful innocence : *White Lilac.*
Youthful love : *Red Catchfly.*

Zealousness : *Elder.*
Zest : *Lemon.*

Z